THE

GHOSTLY TALES

OF

GALVESTON

Published by Arcadia Children's Books
A Division of Arcadia Publishing
Charleston, SC
www.arcadiapublishing.com

Spooky America is a trademark of Arcadia Publishing, Inc.

First published 2021

Manufactured in the United States

ISBN 978-1-4671-9810-3

Library of Congress Control Number: 2021932571

Notice: The information in this book is true and complete to the best of our knowledge. It is offered without guarantee on the part of the author or Arcadia Publishing. The author and Arcadia Publishing disclaim all liability in connection with the use of this book.

All images courtesy of Shutterstock.com; p.42 Everett Collection/Shutterstock.com; p. 48 Kokoulina/Shutterstock.com.

Spooky America

THE
GHOSTLY TALES
OF

GALVESTON

KATHLEEN SHANAHAN MACA

Adapted from *Ghosts of Galveston* by Kathleen Shanahan Maca

arcadia®
CHILDREN'S BOOKS

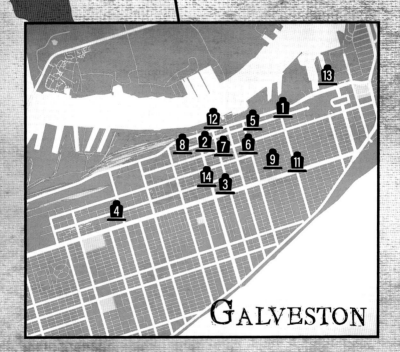

TEXAS

LA   MI   A

GULF OF MEXICO

GALVESTON

TABLE OF CONTENTS & MAP KEY

Galveston

Introduction

Galveston is an island along the coast of Texas, just twenty-seven miles long and three miles wide. Over seven million visitors come to the island every year, and most of them want to play on the beach, tour the old Victorian homes, go shopping, or visit the many museums. But what very few of them know before they arrive is that Galveston is one of the most haunted places in the nation! Need proof? Ask just about anyone you meet there, and it's likely they will have a ghost story to talk about.

Before the city was founded in 1839, the island had already been home to the Karankawa Native Americans, Spanish and French explorers, and countless seafarers, including the infamous pirate Jean Laffite. Laffite wasn't the first pirate to come to the island, but he's definitely the one most people still talk about. He and his men sailed up and down the Texas and Louisiana coasts, capturing Spanish ships and stealing their cargo. Treasure hunters still have never found the loot he supposedly buried beneath three oak trees on the western end of the island. Truth be told, you have a better chance of discovering the ghost of Laffite himself, as you will soon read.

As a port city, Galveston became so prosperous that soon mansions lined Broadway Boulevard, which today is the main drag of Downtown Galveston, just sixty miles south of Houston. However, it could not avoid the peril of the American Civil War. During the Battle of Galveston on New Year's Day in 1863, Confederate troops retook control of the city from Union soldiers. Hundreds of soldiers

from both sides of the conflict were captured, wounded, or killed, and their bodies are buried in the cemeteries on Broadway Boulevard.

By the late 19th century, Galveston had grown into the largest city in Texas. The Strand was the city's center for international trade, and merchants shipped and received goods from all over the world. The access to water made a lot of businesses successful, but it could also bring danger. Being right on the coast of Texas, Galveston was hit by many hurricanes. The worst one struck on September 8, 1900, and is known as the Great Storm. Even now, over 120 years later, that hurricane is considered the deadliest natural disaster in the history of the United States. It killed thousands of people and destroyed two-thirds of the island's homes and businesses. There were so many bodies scattered across the island after the storm that it was hard to know what to do with them. Some were buried where they were found, which means almost anywhere you walk today in Galveston might actually be someone's grave! It's one of the reasons people call Galveston a "cemetery with a beach attached." Other bodies were carried to the Strand, where the dead who weren't recognized by family or friends were taken out to sea on barges and pushed overboard. But just a few days later, the bodies washed back to shore with the tide. Galvestonians had to burn the remaining bodies in funeral pyres, which are like giant bonfires. It was gruesome, but it was their only choice.

As impossible as it seems, Galvestonians recovered after the Great Storm and carried on with their lives. But they never forgot about the island's early tragedies—mainly because the ghosts won't let them. Newspaper accounts describe the ghost of a woman in white who wandered to the piers each night and sightings of apparitions of Union and Confederate soldiers who don't seem to know the war is over—or that they're dead! The ghosts of wealthy businessmen have been reported still guarding their mansions, alongside the spirits of long-lost sailors wandering the ports, waiting for their ships to bring them home at last. They all roam the streets of Galveston, seemingly there from the city's early beginnings and not in any hurry to leave.

Paranormal experts say that spirits can draw strength from water, and if that's true, it makes sense that an island like Galveston is home to so many ghosts. After all, the dead practically outnumber the living on this island. But if you're skeptical so far, read further and decide for yourself what is real and what is not. Just know this: when people ask me if I believe in ghosts, I usually respond by asking, "Have you ever been to Galveston?"

Jean Laffite, the Pirate King

Arrrr, mateys! Pirate ghosts abound in Galveston!

Jean Laffite and nearly 1,000 of his followers arrived on the island in March 1817 and organized a town called Campeche. Now, even though Laffite is known as a pirate, he was actually a privateer. What's the difference, you might ask? Well, not much, except that a pirate worked for himself, while a privateer worked for a government. Laffite worked for the Mexican government, which pretty much just wanted to cause problems for Spanish sailors. Laffite got to keep anything he took from their ships, which was a pretty good deal. Luckily for

his victims, Laffite wasn't violent like many of the pirates we see in the movies, and he'd even let the crews and ships go sometimes once he had their cargo.

Campeche was the perfect spot for Laffite's ships to operate, and soon he built himself a two-story home that he painted red and called Maison Rouge, which is French for "Red House." Laffite filled his mansion with elegant furniture and decorations that his men stole from Spanish ships. The second floor windows of the mansion were used as openings for cannons, which was probably a more effective home security system than any of us have today! But things weren't always smooth sailing for Laffite. In 1818, several of his men were killed in a battle with the native

Karankawa tribe. A hurricane that same year sank four ships in his fleet.

Laffite had married a woman named Madeline Regaud in Campeche, and they had a son named Jean Pierre Laffite, but sadly, Madeline died in 1820, and Laffite was so sad that local stories say he buried her in the basement of his home, surrounded by treasure. Laffite was ordered off the island in May 1821 after his crew raided an American ship—something the US government just wasn't going to put up with. But he didn't leave Galveston without throwing a good ol' pirate-style tantrum! He picked a crew to man his favorite vessel, the *Pride*, then he

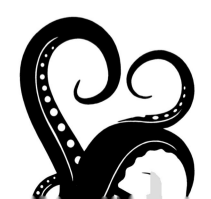

burned down the entire town—including his own Maison Rouge—before sailing away. He was killed in a sea battle off the coast of South America in 1823.

In 1866, a ship captain named Frederick William Hendricks bought the ruins of Maison Rouge. He was a fan of stories about Laffite and wanted to rebuild the home. All that was left was the stone foundation, cellar, and front stairs, but Hendricks used old drawings and descriptions from locals to figure out what Laffite's home originally looked like. Then he built a replica home on top of the ruins and called it Hendrick's Castle. Hendricks and his wife, Kate, died in the late 1880s, and soon after, several people lived in Hendrick's Castle, but never for very long. There just seemed to be too much ghostly activity going on there to stick around.

Though Jean Laffite left the island in 1821, some say that his spirit returned to Galveston. People have seen the pirate's ghost protecting his former home, wearing a red coat and breeches. Some even claimed to have been choked for getting too close him. People passing the ruins of Maison Rouge at night heard unexplained voices, screams, and mumbling when no one was there. On one particular occasion, a woman reported hearing two male voices arguing louder and louder until she ran to get away from the scary sound. Then, in 1907, a woman named Anne Peterson who lived in Hendrick's Castle told friends that she had to move because of the ghosts of pirates. Pirates, it would seem, do not always make friendly roommates.

Hendrick's Castle was torn down in 1952, but you can still see the foundation and stairs on Harborside Drive between Fourteenth and

Fifteenth Streets in Galveston. Today, a local group of history buffs—called the Laffite Society—gather regularly to read and discuss nearly anything to do with their favorite pirate. One Halloween night, members of the Laffite Society got together and held a séance to try to talk to Laffite himself. When one of their members began speaking in tongues—a phenomenon where people mysteriously speak in a language they would not have otherwise known—they decided to never try that again!

Hutchings-Sealy Building

Hutchings-Sealy Building

When they were built in 1895, the Ball, Hutchings & Company Bank and John Sealy Building in the Strand District were referred to as the "Wall Street of the South." This was because so much of Galveston's financial services industry conducted its business there. Today, the building hosts a series of stores, art galleries, and one infamous restaurant, which are packed full with as many ghosts as there are tourists.

During the Great Storm, the waters surrounding Galveston surged, rising seventeen feet above land and flooding the entire first floor of the Hutchings-Sealy Building. As people rushed from every direction to the second and third floors to get away from the endless flooding, a woman the locals refer to as Sara—a heroic young schoolteacher—climbed through a window and stood on a ledge just inches above the raging sea to pull people to safety. With each body she pulled inside,

it became obvious that nearly everyone had drowned. Their bodies were separated from the few who managed to survive on the other side of the floor. The damage done and loss of life were truly devastating.

After the storm passed, Sara stayed at the Hutchings-Sealy Building, taking care of the injured people she rescued. But unfortunately, she became sick a few days later and died in the very same room where her act of extraordinary courage occurred. Her story is one of heroism and tragedy, so it's not surprising that her legend lives long in Galveston. But as you can

imagine by now, that's not the only part of Sara that lives on in the Hutchings-Sealy Building. Her spirit has been seen walking the stairways in a long white dress. Sometimes her voice can be heard whispering in the restaurant on the first floor and the halls on the second floor. The locals say she's still keeping an eye on the building and everyone inside, but she's not alone. The fun-loving spirit of one of her students—one of the many unfortunate souls Sara could not save during the Great Storm— is rumored to haunt a shop called Tina's which is also on the Strand. It is said that though his tale is one of tragedy, nothing could ever take away his playful nature. Not even becoming a ghost.

The women who run Tina's will be the first ones to tell you they often have to pick up the messes made by this mischievous young fellow when the shop closes. Every night before they go home, the employees at Tina's sweep the floors and arrange the countertops of the shop before locking the doors and leaving. But when they open the shop the next morning, things aren't always as neat as they left them. Tina's is famous for their square shaped candles in all sorts of pretty colors. One morning, a candle that had been placed on a shelf several feet away was found right in the middle of the floor. Another time, the young ghost stacked them up like building blocks. But at least moving the candles isn't as messy as when he throws magazines across the floor.

Invisible hands may move things around inside Tina's at night, but the extra cleanup doesn't bother the shopkeepers. They know that he is probably just trying to get attention and doesn't mean any harm. After all, he hasn't ever broken anything . . . yet.

CHAPTER 3

Ashton Villa

Let's take a break from the gruesome tales and hear one about ghosts who know how to have fun!

Along Broadway Boulevard is a giant brick mansion called Ashton Villa. Colonel James Brown, who made his fortune in the hardware business, built it in 1859. At the time, the mansion was considered to be one of the finest homes in the state. Brown's oldest daughter

Bettie was referred to as the "Texas Princess" and was famous for being of an independent mind and spirit—literally!

Bettie loved to travel and find adventure and went to dazzling places like Paris, Morocco, Jerusalem, Egypt, China, and India. She traveled all over the world, studying art and collecting beautiful objects to bring back to Ashton Villa. Bettie also hosted fancy parties and liked to make a grand entrance that people would remember. Once, she arrived with her pet kittens riding on the bottom of her long skirt! Sometimes she even smoked a pipe and played cards with the gentlemen at her parties while other ladies stood by in shock.

One could say that Ashton Villa has lived a life of its own. Its rooms have played host to grand parties, and its halls were filled with music and laughter for many decades. So there's no wonder why it's held in such high regard in Galveston. In 2008, another hurricane—Hurricane Ike—caused terrible water damage to Ashton Villa, and even today, there are still a lot of repairs left to be done. The Galveston Historical Foundation now owns the property and opens it for special occasions, but residents and tourists both look forward to when they can take regular tours of the home again. It's said that the tours of Ashton Villa can be just as lively as some of Bettie's soirees!

Visitors have said they felt like someone was following them around the house during a tour, but no one was there when they turned to look. On another occasion, a tour guide at the home saw a blonde woman in a turquoise ball gown standing at the top of the stairs of the second floor. She was holding an ornate fan, which just happened to be one of Bettie's favorite things to collect. But then, as quickly as she appeared, the apparition then seemed to fade away.

Long ago, that area of the home lead to Bettie's "day room," where she was free to dress informally and relax. A chest of drawers she bought in the Middle East is still in the room and reportedly locks and unlocks by itself. This is even stranger when you realize the key to the chest has been missing for years! The sheets on Bettie's bed always seem to be messed up, too, no matter how often the workers at Ashton Villa straighten them.

But make this note: if you ever have a chance to visit Ashton Villa in the future, and you want to catch a glimpse of the ghost of the Texas Princess, a good date to visit may be February 18—Bettie's birthday. It's said that she usually makes her presence known on this particular day, and rumor has it that, even from the grave, she still loves a good party!

Colonel Brown also had another daughter, Bettie's younger sister Matilda. "Tilly," as she was called, was once married to a local businessman, but unfortunately, their love

was not meant to last. So Tilly and her children moved back into Ashton Villa to live with Bettie.

Tilly could play the piano and violin, and she enjoyed playing music for her family and friends at parties and celebrations whenever she had the chance. That's likely the reason people have said they've heard music echoing from inside the mansion. A caretaker who lived in a carriage house on the property awoke curiously one night to the sound of a

piano. Worried that a burglar had broken into the home, he went to investigate. When he followed the music into the Gold Room, he saw a faint image of a woman in 19th-century clothing playing the piano. Just as he started to say something to her, she faded away.

It's safe to say that until the home is fully open to the public once again, the ladies of Ashton Villa have the grand old mansion to themselves.

CHAPTER 4

Fire Station No. 6

Fighting fires is serious business, but there can be a lot of downtime in between calls to extinguish a dangerous blaze somewhere in town. The ghost of Captain Jack at old Fire Station No. 6 likes to spend his downtime having a little bit of friendly fun.

Galvestonians believe the playful ghost called Captain Jack is the spirit of Captain John "Jack" Knust, who, until his death, worked for the fire department. For nearly forty years, Captain Jack always took good care of the firemen who worked in his crew—and he also liked a good joke.

No. 6 hasn't been a fire station for years. But back when it was still used as an active fire station, the men who worked there had lots of stories to share about weird smells, sounds, and even items disappearing from where people had left them. You have to be brave to be a firefighter, though, and the men who worked at the station weren't afraid of their friendly ghost. But Jack did manage to surprise them every once in a while!

Longtime members of Station No. 6 knew that the cot next to the south window of the firehouse belonged to Captain Jack and didn't dare sleep there. But if a rookie who didn't know better laid down in the captain's favorite spot, he would be shaken by unseen hands until he woke up and moved. They never made that mistake again!

The fun-loving ghost also liked to make the sound of heavy footsteps going up and down the stairway to the sleeping quarters of the firehouse late at night when everyone was in bed. The firemen woke up pretty quick and searched everywhere, but never saw who was walking on the stairs.

Now No. 6 is a church called the Apostolic Firehouse. People say that the captain checks in every once in a while just to make sure things are in order, but nobody really minds. After all, who better to hold watch than a professional? Safety first!

Hendley Row

There are places in Galveston that are so old that the ghosts have been haunting them for generations. Hendley Row is that kind of place. Technically, the row is four separate buildings with a brick front that makes it look like one long building. It took three years to build the sturdy structure, beginning in 1855. When Hendley Row was first built it was used as offices for brothers William and

Joseph Hendley, who were involved in many businesses, including cotton production. You can still see their initials on small grey stones between the tops of the building's windows. A lot of people have come and gone through Hendley Row in the years since it opened, but some have never left.

You remember reading earlier about the Battle of Galveston, right? It took place on the wharf right behind Hendley Row. One of the granite columns from the front side of the building looks as if a piece has been broken off, and that's because it was actually shot off by cannon fire during the battle!

After Confederate general Bankhead Magruder had led his troops in the attack on the Union ships that won Galveston back for the Confederacy, it stayed under their control until the end of the war.

Throughout the war, the buildings were also used as military offices. But during battle, lookouts for both the Union and Confederacy— depending on who was in control of Galveston at the time—used the building to observe enemy troops on land and in the harbor. One of those Confederate soldiers is still on duty today, dressed in his gray uniform.

The staff of the Hendley Market on the first floor, as well as the people who have lived in apartments above, have seen him running up and down the stairs. Maybe he's still rushing urgent messages between the lookout post and his troops. However, he isn't always in a hurry. A few people who have lived in the Row have also heard footsteps across the roof while other Galvestonians have seen the soldier standing next to a doorway holding his rifle like he's on guard duty. Sometimes at night, the soldier can be seen through the shop windows or floating along the roof looking like a white mist in the shape of a man. He must not know the war has been over for over 150 years!

Another mysterious spirit that haunts Hendley Row is the Lady in White. This ghost is often seen in tears, going up and down the stairs, or running back and forth out front as if she were frantically searching for someone. Even when she can't be seen, people have said they've heard her weeping. Because she's described as wearing a white Victorian nightgown or dress, locals think she was one of the many victims of the Great Storm of 1900 and might be searching for a lost loved one.

Wreckage after the Great Storm

Rogers & Nichols Buildings

Across the street from Hendley Row is the Rogers Building. It was built in 1894 but faced grave challenges during its early years. It was damaged by a terrible fire in July 1900 and then again by the Great Storm just two months later. But several merchants still managed to operate their businesses in the Rogers Building through the years, typically a variety of stores that sold goods arriving on the incoming ships, such as liquor.

After the Great Storm, as the citizens of Galveston gathered bodies, they needed a place to put them while they figured out what to do. A now-famous photo was taken of the interior of the Rogers Building, filled with bodies wrapped in sheets. Over one hundred years later, the building is still visited by the spirits of the victims of that terrible tragedy.

Today, the balcony of the Rogers Building is a great place to watch Mardi Gras parades from up above—along with a number of phantoms that have been spotted there for generations, floating across the balcony looking down on people as they pass by. People who work in the building have seen the ghosts of a woman and little boy dressed in old-fashioned Victorian clothing. They are usually seen together, but when the boy is seen alone, he wanders through the upstairs rooms looking sad and confused. But perhaps worst of all, at night, people claim to see visions of the countless dead bodies near the ceiling of the Rogers Building, as though they were floating—or simply trapped. Many believe it is a paranormal rendering of the Great Storm, when waters rose so quickly that bodies of victims were pinned up against the ceilings.

The 1857 E.B. Nichols Building next door is connected to the Rogers Building by an inside staircase and has a reputation for being just as haunted as its neighbor.

Confederate soldiers used to practice their marching formations in the room on the third floor during the Civil War. They must still be practicing, because people hear their footsteps stomping across the floor and walking up and down the stairs. Many ghosts dressed in Civil War uniforms have been seen in both buildings.

Some people see them inside or pacing the sidewalks and streets in front.

The spirit of a little girl named Annabelle is probably the busiest ghost on this side of the street. She can be heard singing in Nichols's back stairwell or sometimes crying softly if she feels frustrated that no one is paying attention to her. She can also find ways to amuse herself and mischievously plays with electronics or opens and closes doors to get the attention she wants.

There is a store named Mysticatz on the first floor of the building now, and the owners have had several experiences with Annabelle. They've even been able to make a video recording of someone—or something—invisible, playing with a pair of pink pliers on their workbench.

The ghosts that call the Rogers and Nichols Buildings home are friendly for the most part. But there is one presence that inhabits the second floor of the Nichols Building who doesn't like to be bothered by the living. He has been known to cause people to feel extremely uncomfortable and panic in order to get them to leave. Nothing is known about him, and no one wants to stay long enough to find out.

THE TREMONT HOUSE

Tremont House Hotel

Tremont House Hotel

The Tremont House Hotel has a very unique history. For starters, it wasn't always a hotel. Since the 1800s, it had been a Civil War outpost, an opera house, and a boarding home before becoming the Tremont House. There have also been three versions of the hotel over the course of Galveston history. The first hotel burned to the ground in a terrible fire, and a second was torn down in 1928. Then in the 1980s, the Blum Building, an old dry goods business, was renamed the Tremont House. A few of the guests at the Tremont House Hotel like it enough to stay permanently—even though they died long ago. Truth be told, nothing is really like a stay at the Tremont Hotel.

Guests and staff of the hotel most often see a Civil War soldier in a Confederate uniform that patrols the lobby, bar, dining, and office areas of the first floor. No one knows who the soldier was, but sightings of him have been recorded multiple times over the last forty years. A long marble hallway stretches from the elevators and past the lobby to guest rooms and offices. Clerks working the front desk sometimes hear the "click, click, click" of boots on the hard floor even when no one can be seen walking by.

The Tremont's beautiful rosewood bar sits at the back of the large lobby. It originally belonged to a French migrant named Henry Toujouse, who used it in his Opera House Saloon in the basement of the Tremont Opera House starting in 1872.

After the opera house closed down in 1894, Henry took the bar across Tremont Street with him and opened Henry's Café at the Stag Hotel. Henry sold his beloved bar and retired in 1913 to spend more time with his wife, Frances. Unfortunately, she passed away four years later. Henry felt lost and alone without his wife and work and took his own life the next year.

His lovely wood bar was found at a local tavern in the 1960s, but it was in bad shape. Luckily it was purchased and restored to its former beauty and installed at the Tremont Hotel. The bar at the Tremont is named Toujouse in honor of its first owner. Many people think that Henry is still keeping an eye on his bar. Guests and members of the staff have witnessed paranormal activity surrounding it almost since the opening day of the hotel.

On Valentine's Day one year, each of the waitresses was given a long stemmed rose by the hotel manager. After they finished work

that night, they gathered around Henry's bar to visit. One of the ladies suggested they leave their roses for the "bar ghost." One of her coworkers laughed at the idea of giving up her flower for what she called a "silly ghost" and laid her rose across the corner of the bar while she reached for her purse. Just then an unseen force chopped the bloom off of the flower, leaving her with nothing but a thorny stem. The other frightened staff members quietly placed their roses on the bar and left as quickly as they could. A word to the wise: don't offend a ghost while sitting at his bar.

The rascal spirit of a boy fondly called "Jimmy" by the staff plays in the kitchen, lobby, elevators, and back alley of the hotel. Like any little boy with a sense of humor, Jimmy likes to play tricks—even if they make a mess.

When glasses move across the lobby bar by themselves and sometimes fall to the floor, Jimmy is the one who gets the blame. People sitting at the bar have seen Jimmy move a glass as far as twelve inches before it stops or falls. Old Henry probably enjoys the company, even though he wouldn't approve of the mess. Jimmy also loves to play tricks on new employees, many of whom claim to have seen the youngster from the corner of their eyes. A new employee was working at the front desk when she saw a young boy playing behind a guest who was checking in to the hotel. When the guest walked away and the boy didn't follow, it felt strange to her. Even more strange, the boy then seemed to suddenly disappear. When she asked the guest about his son, the guest told her he was alone and hadn't seen a child. As it were, it seems that Jimmy was pulling another one of his pranks.

As the Belmont Boarding House, travelers could rent rooms for an extended stay or sometimes just a single night, depending on the duration of their stay. During the 1870s, a salesman named Sam visited Galveston on a business trip. After a full day of appointments, Sam decided to go to one of the local bars and do some gambling. It must have been his lucky night, because by the time he left to go back to his room at the boardinghouse, his pockets were filled with the money he had won. Unfortunately, a lot of people saw how much he won and wanted some of the money for themselves. When Sam arrived on the fourth floor of the Belmont, he was ambushed, robbed, and killed.

To this day, visitors on the east side of the fourth floor of Tremont House report having odd experiences during their stay. One night, the doors to the fourth-floor rooms began to shake, which was followed by a loud pounding, waking everyone on the floor. Then guests reported hearing a strange stomping in the hallway, with a slow dragging noise between each step—like the tired feet of an angry salesman looking for his stolen cash. It might be Sam returning to reclaim what is rightfully his, but no one has ever dared to open their door to take a peek into the hallway to check.

Naturally, you shouldn't believe every story you hear, but when it comes to ghosts, the old saying is true: if you don't have anything nice to say, don't say anything all—because a ghost may come along and take offense. One couple who stayed in room 219 at the Tremont House learned this lesson all too well. They were told about the spirits in the hotel but laughed at the stories. They woke up the next morning and found their clothes pulled out of their suitcases and thrown around the room. The wife's jewelry case, which she locked before going to bed, was also opened, and the key was nowhere to be found. They packed their bags and quickly checked into a different hotel but never laughed at ghost stories again.

CHAPTER 8

Galveston Railroad Museum

There is a big white building at the west end of the Strand known as Shearn Moody Plaza. Part of it was originally the 1913 Union Station that was the headquarters for the Atchison, Topeka & Santa Fe Railroad. There are five train tracks leading up to the back of the building. If you visit the Galveston Railroad Museum, you can see the antique locomotives and railcars and sometimes even take a ride. There are white plaster statues of people inside the lobby of the old depot that locals call the "Ghosts of the Past." But some of the ghosts at the train depot aren't as silent and still as the statues. The most famous ghost at the train station is William Watson, who didn't use the buddy system when he visited the island and ended up losing his head.

Watson came to Galveston on Friday, September 1, 1900, as a crewmember of the steamship Michigan sailing from Brooklyn, New York. It was the first assistant engineer's second voyage, and he was ready for adventure. At eight o'clock that night, he dressed up in his best dark brown coat and pants, a pink and white striped shirt, a black tie, tan shoes, and suspenders. He wanted to look his best while he was exploring the city, and you have to admit, that's a pretty memorable ensemble. However, the last time anyone remembered seeing William Watson in his best threads was two and a half hours later, when two men spotted him walking down Twenty-Ninth Street toward the wharf.

At midnight, switch engine No. 765 was coming up on Twenty-Ninth Street and Avenue A when the foreman on the train saw a body lying on the track. He signaled the engineer to stop, but the engine rolled another twelve feet before the locomotive made a full stop. When the two men got out of the train and walked back to investigate, they found a decapitated body. Without a head, there was no way to

identify the man, but he had been dead less than an hour. An earlier train had killed him, just one block away from his ship.

Police came immediately and wrote down a description of the victim the best they could in the lamplight at night, right down to what color underwear he had on. But no one in the nearby buildings or on the boats at the piers recognized the clothing described by the police.

For nearly three hours, police and railroad crews walked up and down the train tracks until they finally found Watson's head, somewhat remarkably with his hat still on.

His shipmates buried Watson in Lakeview cemetery, but his gravestone was lost a few days later in the Great Storm. Today, no one actually ever sees Watson's spirit—he would be a gruesome ghost without a head—but he definitely makes his presence felt. He is what is known as a poltergeist, or "noisy ghost," that throws and moves things around at the museum and causes strange noises. The creak of doors when they are all closed and locked, the sound of falling items when everything stays in place, or the sound of something (or someone) being hit by something heavy sometimes echo through the waiting room and halls. Watson must be frustrated that he never got to go home.

In the 1990s, the Galveston police department received several telephone calls from the third and fourth floors of the building. When they answered, the only sound the officers heard was heavy breathing. When they played back the recording for clues, they heard faint music playing from the 1920s. Could it have been Watson's ghost playing with the phones? It's quite possible. A paranormal entity certainly inhabits the museum.

Newson House's Ghost Cats

The last thing you might expect to find while you're ghost hunting are the spirits of cats, but in Galveston, anything is possible.

Alfred Newson built a new home at 1801 Ball Street in 1896 with the money he made from his meat market. He lived there with his pet-loving wife Margaret, their daughter Musette, and later, with Musette's husband, George Ketchum.

Now, it would seem only natural that whoever lived in this home through the years might haunt it later. But their pets? Luckily for these spirits, they have the company of their ghostly cats who roam through the pretty Victorian house to keep them company.

A woman who lived in the home at one time found her cat behind the closed door of an upstairs room at the back of the house. She knew that she hadn't been up there in a while, but had seen the cat that morning. How did the cat get in there, and how did the door close? It was a mystery. But the cat seemed perfectly happy to stay in the room.

One of the neighbors later told the lady that was the room of a man who used to live in the house. He was known as a great cat lover and had several of his own. Could it be possible that the ghost of the gentleman wanted to keep his furry company for a while before opening the door?

The same owner, who lived in the home alone, took her dog and cat with her to her bedroom one night and locked the door to get ready for bed. A few minutes later, she heard a loud crash come from downstairs. She carefully walked down the stairs to see what caused the noise and found that a board game she had left in the middle of the table had been flipped over onto the floor. Since her pets were in her room and no one else was in the house, she called the police to help her solve the mystery of how it happened.

When officers interviewed neighbors, one reported he had seen a burglar peeking through the home's window. But whatever the thief saw frightened him so much that he ran away without ever going inside. He must have seen one of the home's protective ghosts show they were there in the best way they knew how. By moving things with unseen hands . . . or paws!

The ghosts in the Newsom home can make themselves helpful in other ways, too. One gentleman who stayed in the home complained that several things had gone missing from his room. He asked out loud that the items be returned and found them all later placed neatly in the center of his bed.

Several former owners of the house have seen cats from the corner of their eyes that disappear when they try to look straight at them. Some have even heard purring or felt the vibrations of purrs. A lucky few have had the invisible resident cats jump onto the furniture and snuggle against them or felt winding soft fur around their ankles at night.

If you pass by the Newson home and spot a large yellow cat sitting in the window or hear a collar bell jingling, just know that they aren't really there. But the ghostly tales (or perhaps we should say *tails*) that come out of the beautiful home on Ball Street would make any animal lover happy.

CHAPTER 10

Stewart's Mansion

An old abandoned white mansion sits out on the west end of Galveston about thirteen miles from the Strand. It's called Stewart's Mansion, and its ghosts and legend date back even further than the building. The graves in the nearby cemetery are only about fifty years old, but spirits have lived there long before that.

About the same time that Jean Laffite built Maison Rouge along the waterfront, he founded a fort and compound on the land where Stewart's Mansion is now. In 1821, Lafitte's men kidnapped a native Karankawa woman, and warriors from her tribe attacked the pirate colony to save her. Five pirates were killed, and the remaining buccaneers took revenge on the tribe by killing most of their men. It was called the Battle of the Three Trees, but since the pirates were the only ones with guns, it wasn't exactly a fair fight.

People who have lived in (or snuck into) Stewart's Mansion say they've seen the spirits of pirates and Native Americans wandering the grounds of the former fort. After dark, the sounds of cannon fire, musket fire, and the blood curdling screams of injured and dying men float across the land.

Lafitte and his men brought slaves with them when they moved to Galveston from New Orleans. Many of these slaves were known to practice voodoo. As fearsome as Lafitte was, it is said that he was afraid of the voodoo practices. That's why he built Maison Rouge at the other end of the island from his colony.

Even now, people claim to hear chanting and the beating of drums around Stewart's Mansion. This part of the island is also known to be the home territory of a pack of twelve phantom black dogs with glowing red eyes known as the Campeche Devil Dogs.

Legend says the dogs were owned by Lafitte himself and bred for hunting down men and animals. Sometimes their spirits are visible. Other times, witnesses only hear the growling, sense the smell of wet dogs, or feel wet fur brushing up against their legs. As if that isn't scary enough, seeing the ghost dogs is an omen that trouble or disaster is about to happen. It is said that they were seen by several Galvestonians just days before the Great Storm, and you've read already about how that turned out.

The paranormal activity that visitors see most often at Stewart's Mansion, however, is harder to explain with stories from history. Eerie, faceless shadow people dash from tree to tree before disappearing inside the mansion. Visitors have heard the sound of children laughing, piano music being played, and loud laughter coming from inside the house when no one is there. For years, the walls inside the mansion were painted with the portraits of pirates in battle. The new owners painted over the frightening artwork, hoping to end the stories that are attached to the land. But even they soon went bankrupt and abandoned the home. Only the terrifying ghosts reside there once again.

Bishop's Palace

Bishop's Palace on Broadway Boulevard looks a bit like a castle, which is probably why tourists take more pictures of it than any other building on the island. Two winged lion statues affectionately called Zeke and Oscar guard the front gate to the mansion and are decorated with bright red bows during the Christmas holidays. Wealthy lawyer and businessman Colonel Walter Gresham and his wife, Josephine, hired the famous architect Nicholas Clayton to design the three-story home. It was so elaborate that it took five years to build. After Colonel Gresham died, his family sold the palace to the Catholic Diocese in 1923, and a bishop lived there for the next forty years. That's when it became known as Bishop's Palace. Today, the palace is owned by the Galveston Historical Foundation and is open for tours.

The Greshams wanted the finest materials from around the world used to build their home. The impressive fireplaces were made of African marble and rare lumber. One is even lined with pure silver. The outside of the mansion is made of three types of stone: granite, limestone, and sandstone. Limestone is one of the natural materials that some people think can hold the energy of spirits, causing what's called residual hauntings. Instead of actual ghosts, this type of haunting is more like a recording of something that happened a long time ago, and someone keeps hitting the replay button.

Sightings at Bishop's Palace may very well be a residual haunting. Locals believe that the combination of the energy of the storm and the limestone in the building cause a replay of Colonel Gresham checking on his home before the Great Storm. During the hurricane, 600 people took shelter with the Greshams in the sturdy mansion and were saved from harm. Today, Gresham is usually seen pacing around the house making sure everything is secure just before storms hit the island. Witnesses have reported that the vision of the former owner walks around the palace, climbs the eighteen stairs to the front porch, paces back and forth around the curved porch, and then disappears through the large wood front doors. With the outside of her mansion safely guarded by her husband, Josephine carries on her activities inside.

A forty-foot tall winding staircase with a domed ceiling surrounded by amber-colored stained glass windows sits at the back of the first floor. Occasionally when the sun is low in the sky, the colored light comes through the windows to make eerie patterns on the dark wood surrounding them, and then an apparition of a woman slowly walks down the stairs. It is probably Josephine, a talented artist in her day whose artwork can still be seen on the walls and ceilings of her home. The Greshams had nine children, and some of her paintings included them. Her art studio was on the third floor and is rarely open for tours. But nonetheless, Josephine is often seen calmly walking past the windows of her workroom enjoying her privacy.

The family loved to have parties for their friends, and one of the items Josephine liked to show to her guests was a large, carved wooden box that stored her postcards from friends and her own travels. The box still sits in a corner of the front room. It is left open so tourists can see the compartments inside and is marked with a strict "do not touch" sign. But the sign must not apply to Josephine, because it isn't unusual for the home's volunteers to arrive in the morning to find it closed or even moved. She should be able to put it where she wants, right? It is hers, after all.

If you're one of the lucky ones, you might spot the spectral images of the entire Gresham family sitting in the sunny conservatory before the figures quickly fade away. It's understandable that they would want to come back and visit their home, where they spent so many happy years.

Haunted Mayfield Manor

There's a fantastic haunted house attraction in Galveston with displays, actors, and all sorts of hidden tricks to scare you. It's not a tour of an old house, it's a fun spooky attraction that was built in the Butterowe Building just off Strand Street. But what the folks who work there found out—and what they don't tell you when you visit—is that the building is actually haunted. It's true!

The old building where the Haunted Mayfield Manor is staged was built in 1885 as a sail-making and furniture factory for the port city. Like the Rogers Building, it also was a staging ground for the dead left in the wake of the Great Storm. Today, visitors are greeted by the wild-eyed fictional character of Dr. Horace Mayfield, who's been driven insane by the number of bodies he needs to deal with. He'll tell you all about it as he leads you through the tour.

The actors and technicians that work at the Mayfield aim to make your experience as

scary and fun as possible. They hide in corners, pop out of secret panels, shoot off air canons, or make portraits seem to come alive at just the right time to make you jump. For most of the actors, their cues come from Dr. Mayfield. They wait to hear him say a particular line or passage, and then—SURPRISE! They reach out from the darkness to grab you! But some actors report that spirits in the building distract and confuse them during tours. Evidently, some of the spirits have heard the tour so many times, they've memorized the lines and whisper them into the ears of the actors early so they mess

up their entrance. Other times, the spirits hold the panels shut so the actors can't get out.

The ghost of a teenage boy is the real prankster of the place. His name is Tom. We know his name because he likes to come and whisper it to ghost hunters who come to explore the Butterowe Building. He's even been known to whisper it into their voice recorders.

Tom likes to play with anything mechanical. He gets a kick out of setting off an air cannon that blows quick gusts of wind at unsuspecting visitors. One time, an employee yelled at him for setting it off in her direction when she knew it was unplugged, and the machine quit working for the rest of the day. Guess even a ghost can get his feelings hurt.

Luckily for Tom, there are plenty of other devices to play with, including a photo booth in the lobby. At night, when no one is in the building, the booth has been known to spit out piles of pictures showing nothing but darkness, except for one eerie time when a blurry face appeared. It happened so often that now the workers unplug the booth before they go home. Sorry about that, Tom.

If you go inside the booth to take a photo on your next visit, don't be surprised if someone or something else shows up in your picture. And if you feel like someone is messing with you the next time you visit the Mayfield, just tell Tom to knock it off. Though, be cautioned that it may not be him. Apparently, Tom has plenty of frightening friends.

Doors seem to open and close by themselves thanks to a spirit named Ben, a ghost who really, *really* likes doors. Ben likes to lock people in or out of the bathrooms, and he really made people jump one time when he shook the bathroom handle hard as if someone was trying to get out. When the tour guide opened the door no one was inside. Workers also think he's the reason why a heavy elevator door often opens by itself repeatedly. There is also Judith, the transparent phantom who can make cold breezes blow and also likes to whisper into visitors' ears. The neat thing about Judith, though, is she's so crafty and quick, visitors sometimes do not realize until later that she isn't meant to be part of the production!

The Face

Ask anyone in Galveston if they've seen "the Face," and they will know just what you're talking about. It's the image of an unidentified man that seems to be haunting the campus of Ewing Hall at Galveston's University of Texas Medical Branch (UTMB, for short)—and no one can convince him to move.

Ewing Hall has a strange feature that the architect *definitely* didn't plan. The huge face of a man glares out from a wall facing the waters of the bay. No one quite remembers when the face appeared the first time, but every local has seen it. The eyes, mouth, and nose might

be caused by dark stains or watermarks on the concrete, or they might be something much more frightening.

It was originally spotted on a concrete block up high above the ground. When rumors started to spread about the face, the university worried that people would trespass on the property to see it, and the solution seemed simple: they decided to get rid of it.

The school sandblasted the image off of the concrete block and thought the problem was solved. But the Face has a strange habit of reappearing. When the concrete dried, the Face had moved to the concrete block right below where it was before.

When word got out that the Face had moved, UTMB had trouble keeping teenagers, ghost hunters, and paranormal investigators away from the building. So they tried again, but their efforts were in vain. The school removed the image one more time, and—just as it had before—it moved one more block lower. It was as if the menacing Face was taunting anyone who tried to make it go away. The image has stayed in that same space for years now, and the university has given up on trying to erase it. Some people say that's because it isn't worth the effort. Others think there's a fear that the next time, the Face will slip inside the door right below where it is currently and go inside the building.

There are all kinds of theories about whose face it might be. Maybe a man who was cheated out of his land or someone with a grudge against the university or hospital. But, in truth, there's really no telling who it is. You'll have to see it and decide for yourself.

But wait! The building is on private property, so the best way to see the Face is to take a harbor boat tour. Guides on the tours are happy to point out the wall from a safe distance aboard their boats, because at least for now, the unidentified Face continues its gaze into the Gulf.

Rosenberg Library

Libraries are a great place to find books filled with stories about ghosts, especially around Halloween. But Galveston's Rosenberg Library has a ghost of its own.

Frank Patten was the first head librarian at Rosenberg when it opened in 1904, and he worked there for over thirty years. The library didn't have a big budget, and when they couldn't afford new books, Patten bought them with his own money. He even secretly donated money during hard times to make sure the assistant librarians were paid.

He personally chose all of the books for the children's section, which was his favorite place to spend time. Patten enjoyed visiting with the kids who visited the library so much, he even started a summer reading club for the months when kids in Galveston were out of school.

Patten passed away in 1934 at the age of seventy-eight, but his library is still here.

Regular visitors to the children's section know there is more than one reason to mind their manners during their stay. Children who mistreat books or roughhouse in the children's section sometimes receive a little thump on their shoulder or heads from an invisible hand. It's Patten's way of reminding them to behave. After all, he paid for many of the books himself. Faint, ghostly laughter of children has been heard echoing up and down the staircases, and perhaps they're spirits returning to a place where they had so much fun.

After the doors are locked for the night, security guards and cleaning crews hear

footsteps on the marble floors. And every once in a while, unexplained footsteps and dragging noises come from the attic, where old paintings, furniture, and other items from the past are stored. A few artifacts from an Egyptian tomb, including a mummy's headrest, are stored in the same space. When the guards go upstairs

to investigate, nothing is out of place. Maybe Patten is still organizing his collections.

If you visit Rosenberg library and catch a glance of a grey-haired gentleman in a suit walking the halls or climbing the stairs, it's only Patten keeping an eye on his beloved library, making sure that things are in order and the visitors are happy.

CHAPTER 15

The Future Is Unwritten

Our journey through the spooky island banks of Galveston ends where it began, with a simple question: "Do you believe in ghosts?" To which I reply, "Do you believe in the power of possibility?" Even with all of its rich history buried in the sands of time, Galveston gives you a feeling that the best is yet to come. There are many things about modern Galveston that offer great promise and prosperity on this sunny island.

Now, after reading about supernatural pirates or spirits in the material world still trapped within history's natural disasters—not to mention all the bodies piled high to ceilings—it would be understandable if your head was spinning, just like our friend William Watson's did when he made a fateful date with a roaring locomotive!

But those locomotives, as well as the ships that grace the harbors of the city, and the many apparitions and poltergeist we have met on this journey, have all played a role in what has made Galveston the thriving and intriguing city that it is today—even if it is truly a "cemetery with a beach attached."

So come to Galveston and experience all the life, and afterlife, that the city has to offer. You might stumble across Jean Laffite's lost riches or even Laffite himself. Check into the Tremont House Hotel and try to catch a glimpse of Henry Toujouse guarding over his beloved bar. And should you run into Bettie, be sure to tell her that her insistence on being independent will remain an inspiration to both the living and the dead forever.

If nothing else, the next time someone asks you if you believe in ghosts, you can reply,

"Have you ever been to Galveston?"

Kathleen Shanahan Maca lives in Clear Lake, Texas, and works on Galveston Island writing about its history. A graduate of Sam Houston State University, she is the author of *Galveston's Broadway Cemeteries* from Arcadia Publishing, and a member of the Texas Chapter of the Association for Gravestone Studies. A fan of ghost stories and legends since she was a child, she uses her experience in historical research and genealogy to add dimension to local folklore.

Check out some of the other Spooky America titles available now!

Spooky America was adapted from the creeptastic Haunted America series, for adults. Haunted America explores historical haunts in cities and regions across America. Each book chronicles both the widely known and less-familiar history behind local ghosts and other unexplained mysteries. Here's more from *Ghosts of Galveston* author Kathleen Shanahan Maca:

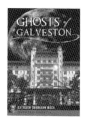

www.kathleenmaca.com